SEARCHER

SEARCHER

An Almost A-Z of Poems

by

Judith Nicholls

THE HOBNOB PRESS

2022

First published in the United Kingdom in 2022

by The Hobnob Press,
8 Lock Warehouse, Severn Road, Gloucester GL1 2GA
www.hobnobpress.co.uk

British Library Cataloguing in Publication Data
A catalogue record for this book is available from the British Library

ISBN 978-1-914407-42-0

Typeset in Adobe Garamond Pro 12/14 pt.
Typesetting and origination by Loren Ryland-Epton

Cover illustration, frontispiece and all drawings by Judith Nicholls

*For all my family, with much love
and remembering John,
always*

CONTENTS

TELL ME A TALE

LISTEN! Open your ears and your dreams
as you step into forests of old,
to distant lands of dragons,
of princes and pots of gold . . .
Open your dreams to the whispering spells
as the magic tale is told.

ACORN

Acorn
egg-in-cup,
dizzy drop
seed side up
on the forest floor.

Winter.
Wet then warm,
sun and storm,
acorn gone,
tree is born,
oak stands there once more.

ALL ABOARD!

Hurry! cried Noah,
and into the ark
rushed

the osprey and the otter
the ostrich and the ox,
the jackal, kangaroo and kite
the scorpion and the fox.
The cacomistle, fresh from sleep
inside his hollow tree,
the cockroach and the cockatoo
the whistling chickadee.
The leopard and the tiger
the squat-nosed liverfluke,
the slow-worm and the glow-worm
and the shy young snake-eyed sheik.
Hinny, hippo, hobby,
hyena, hare and horse,
they all rushed over Noah's plank
before the storm broke loose.

Come in, come in! cried Noah,
Firefly, light these cloudy skies!
In crept grass-snake and glass-snake,
begging birds and mice.

Welcome mealybug and barnacle
and you too, leaf-nosed bat!
Do watch the step – our table's set,
the meal is steaming hot.
I only hope – these skies are black –
our simple ark won't fail!

The swan flew in disdainfully
with Chinese-painted quail.

Oh firefly, light our cloudy skies!
Do come in, mole, and rat.
If God is willing, here's your home
beside Mount Ararat.

AND HOW ARE YOU . . . ?

How am I?
I'm not so bad,
the ankle's just about all right
(except at night)
but shoulder . . .
that's a different tale.
You hadn't heard? It was a nasty fall!
I went with quite a whack,
quite set me back –
I've never *known*
such throbbing!
Lucky not to smash the bone.
But still . . .
   I mustn't moan.

Of course,
this sinusitis doesn't help!
They did my nose last year, you know.
I'll never breathe the same!
Then tonsillitis
and a nasty bout of 'flu . . .
What can you do,
I ask myself,
when you're alone?
The family's gone,
all moved from home.
I wish . . . but no,
   I mustn't groan.

You're going away?
I'd like to go, of course,
but with *my* legs . . .
I never stray too far.
You see that nasty scar

where they tied up the vein?
You'd never *dream*
there'd be such pain
from such a simple job.
But otherwise . . .
    I can't complain.

A LINCOLNSHIRE CHILDHOOD

She seldom left the house,
my grandmother.
Oh, she padded to the barn,
gave orders to my father,
worn from sawing musty logs –
and even bats lay low
above her thankless tongue,
 rising in twilight musk.
Only her step was muffled
by slippers, sought each Christmas
worn inside and out.
Shoes stayed paper-stuffed,
reserved for funerals and the like,
no doubt.

Monday brought steaming sheets
and tempers, brandished dollylegs
and mangled bloomers,
chaste from copper tubs.
Twin lav, piled high
with last month's dusty *Mails*,
was once more freshly-scrubbed,
though even Co-op bristles
never quite removed
the stench of chamber pots.

Linen sheets, now peasant white,
flounced boldly, barn to wall;
inside, zinc bath
half-full of pan-warmed water
circled child and man alike.
And half a lifetime on

they shiver,
wait in silent childhood dreams
the drama of her entrances.

*('Dollylegs' can now be seen in folk museums: a kind of
small wooden stool with four legs on the end of a long-
handled stick. They were used to agitate the washing in the
huge copper boiler.)*

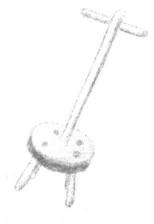

ARS MATHEMATICA

Any
triangle
with two equal angles
of however many degrees you please
will be known by the grand name of isosceles.

Parallelogram
not a problem
a rectangular,
dipsomaniacal
quadrilateral.
Right angles?
Not necessary.
Systematical!
So ecstatical,
problematical
box that I am,
parallelogram!

A trapezium.
Here is an easy one
two sides are parallel
this you can follow well
two more can be symmetrical
result can even be poetical!

A
square
is four-sided
completely right-angled
nothing new-fangled
or rare in a
square

.

Next
the hexagon.
Here's a pesky one
six axes of symmetry
so handy in geometry
tessellates simply
polygon for
six.

You have certainly seen a rectangle,
if you've ever been in a quadrangle
four sides and equal sides opposite
four right angles – not my favourite.

ANNE BOLEYN

Would you like to be a queen
with a crown upon your head?
Would you join the king in court,
and share the royal bed?

Would you like to be a queen,
to spread your wit and charm,
with a crown upon your head . . .
and your head beneath your arm?

BALLAD OF THE SAD ASTRONAUT

Why are you weeping, child of the future,
For what are you grieving, son of the earth?
Acorns of autumn and white woods of winter,
Song-thrush of spring in the land of my birth.

You have a new life, child of the future,
Drifting through stars to a land of your own.
With Sirius to guide you, Orion beside you
Wandering the heavens you are free from earth's harm.

I have a new life, the speckled skies' beauty,
Left far behind me the dark cries of earth;
Oh, but I long for the soft rains of April,
Ice-ferned Decembers and suns of the south.

What was I dreaming, to drift with Orion,
To leave for cold Neptune my home and my hearth?
Stars in their millions stretch endless, remind me
Far far behind lies my blue-marbled earth.

Here on the hillside the dawn is just rising,
Buttercups dew-fill, all silken and gold.
Well may you weep, sad child of the future,
Well may you yearn for your beautiful world.

ARRIVAL OF THE ENVELOPES

Each Christmas they arrive,
drop guilt through my letterbox
like uninvited guests:
a festive season's tax
against excess.

Later, coffee-stained
among the shopping lists
they steal into my mind:
what price a baby,
out of sight
in some forgotten land . . .
or Christmas tree, a turkey, wine?
Uneasily I waver,
choices intertwined.

Next day I gather
in a rush of shame
worn shirts and unworn shoes
for Christmas sales;
cook leftovers,
walk into town.
Though skies are grey
I don't complain;
patiently, for once,
peg blankets out to dry,
remembering some child
with no wrap to his name
who waits, more patiently than I
beneath a different sky
for rain.

Each Christmas,
bellies overfed again
we reach, shame-faced,
for cheque or purse.
Each Christmas we recall
with just a twinge of pain,
a child who lies,
belly distended,
with no crust to his name;
who starves,
who dies.

BAMBOOZLED!

A polar bear just loves an icy landscape,
The eagle likes a mountain with a view;
A whale demands an oceanful of water . . .
All *I* want is a thicket of BAMBOO!

The magpie gathers sticks and straw for nesting,
For a woodlouse some rotting bark will do;
The rabbit digs her home beneath the forest . . .
For *mine* I just need old stalks of BAMBOO!

Some tasty mouse is buzzard's choice for dinner,
A field of grass is what a cow will chew;
Koalas can't resist their eucalyptus . . .
All *I* need is a bunch of ripe BAMBOO!
Please!

BIRTH DAY
1st July 1967

I have been happy here, still safely curled
within my watery cave of endless night;
but time has come to leave this floating world.

My life is one of sound, by moon-tides lulled
here in my inland sea, in dream-filled flight;
I have been happy here, still safely curled.

I have danced, spiralled, somersaulted, twirled,
felt new limbs strengthen, reach like soaring kite –
but time has come to leave this floating world.

Voices seep through my boundaries, ocean-dulled;
I punch my greeting, now with growing might.
I have been happy here, in safety curled.

And yet . . . I am confined, imprisoned. Life is walled
in darkened space, constricting now, too tight;
the time has come to leave my floating world.

Heart leaps, breath catches; I am thrust, drawn, hurled
into my father's hands and dazzling light.
I have been happy here, in safety curled . . .
But now life beckons: *'Leave this floating world!'*

BLUEBOTTLE

Who dips, dives,
swoops out of space,
a buzz in his wings
and sky on his face;
now caught in the light,
now gone without trace,
a sliver of glass,
never still in one place?

Who's elusive as pickpocket,
lord of the flies;
who moves like a rocket,
bound for the skies?
Who's catapult, aeroplane,
always full-throttle?
Sky-diver, Jumping Jack,
comet, *bluebottle!*

BODYWORK

Fibula, tibia, tarsals and rib,
clavical, cranium, spine;
whatever the outside appearance,
all praise to the inner design!

I've a mandible, patella, metatarsal,
I have biceps, I have triceps and a brain;
a pulmonary artery takes blood one way,
then back it comes through pulmonary vein.
There's retina and anvil, epiglottis,
oesophagus and pancreas and tongue;
how could I cope without my parathyroids,
Eustachian tube or diaphragm or lung?

Fibula, tibia, tarsals and rib,
clavical, cranium, spine;
whatever I seem from the outside,
you can't fault the inner design!

CALIBAN'S CAVE

The sand is damp
and cold as stone
when the tide creeps back
from Caliban's Cave.

The rocks are black
as you creep alone
on the dark, damp sand
of Caliban's Cave.

The seagulls sing
and the sea-shells moan
as they slide in the tide
through Caliban's Cave.

The pebbles ring
like the crack of a bone
as you tiptoe deep
into Caliban's Cave.

The music dies
when the waves have gone
and you stand alone
in Caliban's Cave.

You stand in the heart
of Caliban's Cave . . .

CAROUSEL:
the horse's song

An untamed spirit in disguise,
though I'm no rebel runaway
yet still I reach for soaring skies.

I have my lows, I have my highs,
as any long-time captive may;
an untamed spirit in disguise.

No winds will ever hear my sighs
for sighs and cries are not my way,
but still I reach for soaring skies.

Though tethered tightly from sunrise
I dance with joy through blue or grey,
an untamed spirit in disguise.

The circling world spins past my eyes,
a potpourri of disarray:
I only reach for soaring skies.

Escape, maybe, would be unwise
but dreams like mine will not decay;
an untamed spirit in disguise,
one day I'll reach the soaring skies.

CHRISTY'S RAP

There's a boy down at the pool who said he couldn't
        swim;
First he didn't want to go then he wouldn't get in . . .
Now you won't believe it but that boy is so cool,
He's the meanest, keenest swimmer in the local
        swimming pool.
With a dip, dart, glide and slide,
Slither, slather, splish!

There's a boy down at the pool who wouldn't swim on
        his back;
First he wouldn't try, then one day he got the knack.
Now you won't believe it but that boy is like a fish,
He's the meanest, keenest swimmer who'll swim any
        stroke you wish.
With a dip, dart, glide and slide,
Slither, slather, splish!

There's a boy down at the pool who would never try
        the jumps,
Then one day he took a deep breath and quickly came
        up trumps.
Now you won't believe it but you cannot keep him
        out;
He's the meanest, keenest swimmer without any drop
        of doubt!
With a dip, dart, glide and slide,
Slither, slather, splish;
With an under, over, curve and swerve . . .

That boy thinks he's a fish!

CIRCUS ELEPHANT

Today, I dance,
I tiptoe, sway,
with sawdust at my knees;
yesterday, lifetimes away,
I lumbered through the trees.

CLOWN

Pocketful of water-pistols,
eggs to bounce or throw or drop;
bucketful of spilling water,
pants that droop and shoes that flop.
Broken ladder, stilts, a bike
without a seat and just one wheel . . .

Does he *really* like being laughed at,
underneath his painted smile?

COCKROACH

Scuttle-bug,
shadow-foot,
bringer of night;
sky without stars,
obsidian-light;
shiny as coal,
new-mined and still bright;
smooth as new carbon,
dark and untyped.

DANDELION IN WINTER

Where now, my
sleepyhead, old lion's teeth,
bold wet-the-bed?
Sly stowaway, why hide away
your golden wine
till leafy May?
No mirrored stars
for chill December fields?
Where did it go,
your time-tell summer snow
now winter's come?
Your molten suns
lie buried, cold
and yet . . .
you whisper
from your silent world,
volcano-rumbles
caging summer power.
A thousand traitors
lurk in earth's damp cellar,
wait till March gives in;
then every spring . . .
You win, you win, you win!
My phantom sower,
sparkler-shower,
heart-of-iron,
dandelion!

DOLPHIN DANCE

We are darters and divers
from secret sea-caves.
We're dippers and gliders,
we dance through the waves.

We spiral and curl,
we weave as we fly,
stitch shimmering arches
from ocean to sky.

DRAGONBIRTH

In the midnight mists
of long ago
on a far off mountainside
there stood
a wild oak wood . . .

In the wild, wet wood
there grew an oak;
beneath the oak
there slept a cave
and in that cave
the mosses crept.
Beneath the moss
there lay a stone,
beneath the stone
there lay an egg,
and in that egg
there was a crack.
From that crack
there breathed a flame;
from that flame
there burst a fire,
and from that fire

dragon came.

DREAM JOURNEY

Open eyes wide,
gaze into the wind.
Stare at sea or land,
leave thoughts behind.
Most of all, *don't talk!*
Soon you will see inside . . .

Now, let your mind
take you for a walk!

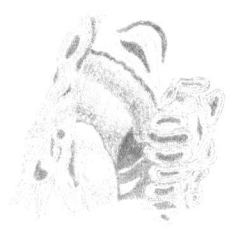

DRAGON NIGHT

A dragon creeps
into my head
and wanders,
stealthy as a moon,
when day is left behind.
At dead of night,
as light as air,
as dark as lead
she sneaks,
in silence;
creeps into my head,
into my mind.

A dragon prowls
into my mind
and presses,
silent as a star,
into my dreams.
When day is left behind,
on padded feet
she treads through darkness,
pressing, pressing,
silently she presses
through the forests
of my mind.

A dragon roars
into the night,
hurls flames,
as fiery as a sun,
before my eyes, behind;
scours shadows into life
and thunders, panting
fire that sets alight

the forests of my dreams.
The dragon roars
into my night,
into my mind.

DUSK

The beach has cleared.
All but a stalwart few
(young sweethearts,
tramps or local dogs)
have emptied shoes
of stones and sand,
retreated to the prom.
With hands and spirit warmed
by local fish and chips,
each one reviews his day.

The sun is low across the bay,
changes the shape of things,
casts magic over what was not.
The beach-day's litter
fades into a kindly gloom;
the clock-tower, dull at noon,
now turns to magic Camelot
and visions of enchanted nights
are stirred as, one by one,
a thousand wandering stars
give way to endless lights.

EARTH RIDDLES

Painted glass bauble,
swung on an unseen thread.

Curled palette of light,
splashed on dark canvas.

Lapis lazuli,
brush-stroked with white.

Lone marble,
rolled over threadbare velvet.

A medal,
pinned to the blue blazer of night.

Space-hopper,
cast like a kite over silent seas.

Small change
in a deep pocket.

EARTHSET

Night spreads like purple heather
over wasteland sky
and marbled earth rolls gently into sleep.

ELEGY

'Mummy, what was an elephant?'

Each ear was tuned to the forest,
each trunk uncurled to the sun;
each forehead domed against a sky
unchanged since time began.

Each head was raised in greeting
as they swayed from each new dawn,
and the timeless paths of the forest
echoed with trumpet-song.

Now the skies are dark,
the paths have gone;
what once was a forest
has turned to stone.
Now only vultures
shadow the sky
and the queens of the forest
are left, to die.

Before we are silenced,
hear our song;
before we are silenced,
hear our cry.

EYE OF THE STORM

The great sea painter J.M.W. Turner once had himself
lashed to a ship's mast in order to experience a storm at sea.

Spray lifts and hovers,
soon whisked white
from darkening seas.
Sails strain before the mast;
with each new gust
taut riggings groan.
Wind rises still,
prises eyelids open,
claws at cheeks and nostrils
sharp with salt.

Vertical is lost;
she rolls and pitches,
pitches, rolls.
And mast and man lurch on
as one, through sea and air;
through gloom then glare,
they twist into the staring eye
of Turner's first sea-storm.

Sky breaks all round;
green light dissolves grey noon,
day becomes night.
The weight of waters,
lava-angry,
churns beneath, around.
The seagulls' cry is lost
as ocean rises up to meet the sky.

Waves curve
and swell, mast-high,
to spinning walls
of foam and cloud and ocean.
Keel swerves and lifts,
dragged to the peak
then spewed down concave cliff
to beckoning trough beneath,
skewed in the undertow.

Gunwales dip to starboard,
mast falls, a hinging lid
to close the gaping sea below.
But no, she rises;
counter-balanced,
lists to port,
is tossed head-on,
the sport of some sea-god,
towards another wave
above the surging foam.

~ ~ ~ ~ ~

And he,
transfixed with fear and cold,
still stares.
Through artist's eye, salt-stung,
he fixes in his head
the green eye of the storm;
and even as his life is hurled
to places out of time,
where earth and sea and sky are one,
holds still the moving image in his soul;
later, recreates it whole
and pours it on to canvas
for the world.

EVOLUTION

I met my foe the other day;
we fought with fist and knee.
We grappled, shouldered,
kicked and roared
till finally, our limbs subdued,
each slunk away.

I met my foe the other day;
he came with fist
and I with sword.
I answered flesh
with sharpened steel,
he sank without a word.

I met my foe the other day;
I brought my dainty gun.
He bared his sword to greet me;
one finger crooked,
my foe was gone.

I saw my foe the other day –
no more than just a blur
across a smoky battlefield.
I saw him fall . . .
        or was it *her?*

I didn't even see my foe –
no faces, no distress.
I pressed the button quickly
and found a wilderness.

FIGHTING SLEEP

Bed!
they said.
I'll never sleep!
I whined . . .

But then,
somehow, I find
sleep creeps
into my mind.

For goodness sake,
I'm wide awake!
I lie.
Sleep stares me in the eye.

I try
to raise my head,
to slide down from my bed.
My back is lead.

N – O – W!
sleep sighs
and gently closes
both my eyes.

FIRELIGHT

Last night,
as flames curled round my coal,
I thought I saw,
a million years ago,
a forest fall.

FIRST TELEVISION

It was 1953.
My dad had won the pools:
some pounds and shillings spare!
He'd buy our first TV.

Coronation coming up,
chance of a lifetime!
he cried excitedly.
I never thought we'd see!

And he,
abandoning his much-loved wireless,
settled down to dream in black and white
of London pomp.

On Coronation Day
I did begin to watch,
to please my dad . . .

But back in school,
to celebrate, they'd handed out
free tickets for the fair.
It wasn't long before
I grew impatient,
tired of moving images,
seen from a lolling chair.
And drawn instead by dodgems,
ghost trains, candy floss,
I walked out on those early pictures
snatched from air.

FISHING SONG

Ragworm, lugworm, mackerel, maggot,
Grey pike lurking, still as steel.
Cast my rod in the deep dark stream
With a nugget of bread for a silver bream.

                                     Caught an eel.

Ragworm, lugworm, mackerel, maggot,
Number Ten hook and I'm waiting still.
A carp would be good or a spiny perch,
A golden rudd or a red-finned roach?

                                             It's an eel.

Rag-worm, lugworm, mackerel, maggot,
Something's biting, wind up the reel!
Is it a pike or a roach or a rudd?
A hunting gudgeon from the river bed?

                                           Just – an eel.

FOR A NEW-BORN CHILD

Welcome to the world!
May loving hands calm your cries
and cradle your waking;
may they stroke away fear,
shelter and hold you,
rejoice in your making;
each night may they silently
guard and enfold you
curled in your sleep;
may they always keep you
safe in your world.

FORTY-ONE

The door is locked,
the curtains drawn;
the paint has peeled
from years of sun.
But there's no-one dare
play 'knock and run'
or stand and stare
at forty-one!

For old Mr. Dunn
of forty-one
is never seen
till the sun has gone.

There's no letter-box
at forty-one;
no postman knocks
for Mr. Dunn.
There's nobody knows
just what goes on
in the silent rooms
of forty-one.

For old Mr. Dunn
of forty-one
is never seen
till night has come.

'There's *nobody* there
at forty-one!'
some may declare;
but I know they're wrong.
For a grey cat prowls
across the lawn

and I've seen a light
where the curtain's torn;
and a shadow creeps
beneath the moon
when midnight strikes
at forty-one.

For old Mr. Dunn
of forty-one
steals out of his house
when midnight's come . . .

FUTURE PAST

Lord of Africa,
swaying giant of the plains;
tree-mover,
sand-tosser,
diviner of water
from the dry river bed:
where are you now?

Where is the song on ivory keys
that echoed through the dusk?
The song's cut away
for a handful of beads,
which once were a living tusk.
Now only baubles
glint in the sun,
for the forest lord fell
to the sound of a gun.

GOODWIN SANDS

I have seen the pale gulls circle
against a restless sky;
I have heard the dark winds crying
as dusk-drawn clouds wheel by.

But the waiting waves still whisper
of shadowy ocean lands,
of twisting tides and of secrets
that lie beneath the Sands.

I have seen the wild weeds' tangle
and smelt the salted squall;
I have seen the moon rise from the seas,
and felt the long night's fall.

But whose are the voices that echo
from the shifting ocean lands,
that tell of secrets buried
beneath the drifting Sands?

For many sail the Goodwins
and some return to shore;
but others ride in the falling tide
and those are seen no more.

And voices rise from the waters
beneath a restless sky:
in the dying light of coming night
the long-lost sailors sigh;
from the watery lands of Goodwin Sands
I hear the sailors cry.

GRACE

It is no night for journeys.
Winds whine their way into a steady roar,
claw bellyfuls of ocean
into watery walls before us.
Dizzily we rise,
plunge into troughs below,
rise again, grip oars,
and gasp for breath.
Cloud glowers all around,
dragged down to melt in spray;
beneath, the waiting ocean lies,
demanding, ever-hungry,
dark as death.

It is no night for journeys
yet . . . somehow the boat,
enfolded like a wayward child
by loving, unseen arms,
holds fast beneath the starless night.
Between the thunder-roll of waves
and lashing sea-salt blurring sight
we hold our course,
believing only in
a safe return to light.

It was no night for journeys.

HAIR-RAISER

Why are there hairs in your nose, Daddy;
why all those hairs in your nose?
Those are vibrissae, my darling;
vibrissae, as everyone knows!

Why are there hairs on your chest, Daddy;
why are there no hairs on mine?
Hairs on your chest will come later, my son;
hairs on the chest take some time!

Why's there no hair on your head, Daddy;
why not a hair on your head?
Hair on the head is an optional extra –
now eat up your dinner, then *bed!*

HARVEST HYMN

We plough the fields and scatter
our pesticides again;
our seeds are fed and watered
by gentle acid rain.
We spray the corn in winter
till pests and weeds are dead –
who minds a little poison
inside his daily bread?

All good gifts around us
beneath our ozone layer
are safe, oh Lord,
so thank you Lord
that we know how to care.

HERMITAGE WOODS

Who was the hermit of Hermitage Woods,
and why did he walk alone?
Was his bed of moss and his roof a star,
was his pillow stone?

Was the hoot of the owl his lullaby,
the wind in the oak his song?
Was the moon his only candle,
when day was done?

Who was the hermit of Hermitage Woods,
and why was he there?
When he smiled, who shared his laughter;
when he cried, who could hear?

Was the scent of pine in his winter breath?
Did his eyes burn with the sun?
What taste of mists swirled in his throat
and round his tongue?

Who *was* the hermit of Hermitage Woods,
who walked at dusk and dawn?
Where are the oaks which sheltered him?
Where has he gone?

HOW THE TORTOISE GOT ITS SHELL

Come to my feast!
cried the great god Zeus.
Today I shall be wed!
And from each corner of the earth
all Zeus's creatures sped . . .

The fliers and the creepers,
the long, the short, the tall;
the crawlers and the leapers,
the feathered, furred and bald;
hunters, biters, finders, fighters,
hooters, whistlers, roarers;
squeakers, screamers, squawkers, dreamers,
nibblers, gulpers, borers.
Paws and claws from hills and shores,
from south, from north, from west and east,
from mountain tops and forest floors
all Zeus's creatures joined the feast
except
                                    the tortoise.

They raved, they pranced, they feasted, danced;
six days and nights each creature stayed
to chatter, flatter, clap and cheer
at the great god Zeus's grand parade
except
                                    the tortoise.

Next day . . .
Why weren't you there, my friend, asked Zeus,
the day that I was wed?

The tortoise smiled her small, slow smile
and raised her small, slow head.

A wedding feast is fun, I guess,
but I'm a simple one.
I'm happy by myself, she said.
There's no place quite like home!

How dare you stay away! roared Zeus.
I'll show you just what for!
From this day on you'll carry your home
on your back, for evermore!

HOW TO EAT A STRAWBERRY

First, sniff –
and then a deep inhale;
note the saliva-flood
round tooth and gum.

Observe seed-studded red,
then feel: Braille promises
through fingertip and thumb
of tastes to come.

Next – bite;
sink deep incisors
into silken flesh –
let juices run!

Close lips;
grasp, roll the prize
through darkened cave
with curling tongue.

Now – *crush*!
Squeeze, savour, pause;
let juice and pulp invade each cell
with taste of summer sun . . .

until the first fruit's gone.

Now take another one!

IN PRAISE OF AUNTIES

An aunt
is a tender plant.
You really can't
be too fond of an aunt.

JACK'S TALE

'At day-break, Jack finding the Giant not likely to be soon roused, crept softly out of his hiding-place, seized the hen, and ran off with her.'
        Iona & Peter Opie: The Classic Fairy Tales

Sun rises before me,
dazzles pathless flight.
In the corner of each eye
mists drift and fade,
dissolve against a lightening sky;
the tops of oaks sprawl
like giant undergrowth below.
I dare not pause to gaze,
I dare not fall!

Behind, as if in smoke,
the castle disappears.
My life is ruled by noise:
heart drums inside my chest,
the giant thud of angry steps
invades my ears.

Beneath one arm
a squirming weight of feathers,
crooked between waist and elbow,
squawks our whereabouts into the dawn;
scratches tales of panic into flesh.
All thoughts are on escape;
all golden dreams have flown!

Ahead, at last,
green stalks emerge from cloud
then cobweb downwards,
stitching earth to sky.

I leap, grasp branches urgently
with outstretched hand;
half-slide, half-fall
to blessed earth below,
to blessed land.

JAIRUS' DAUGHTER

Rush presses at my back,
distracts from smell of bread,
hot women, dust.
Wailing drifts over with dovecall,
donkey's bray
and rustling fig.
Through closed eyes I know
my father's stoop,
my mother's woe.

Sun splinters
the narrow lattice,
fills the room;
slowly reaches
hand and hair and eyes.
Hush falls like a mist
on all the women round.
Morning has come;
I reach,
I rise.

JONAH'S LAMENT

Dark, only dark,
with only hands for eyes;
saved – for a life of touch!
Is *this* my end,
fumbling at some bony stalactite
inside this dank, rank cave?
What scaffold props my roof,
curves out damp walls,
all velvet-hung?
Moist flesh,
indenting to my touch,
closes like giant clam,
a curling tongue.
Some swallowed, mucus-tacky fish
noses its scaly length about my neck,
lost in the slap of falling sea.
Salt rinses mouth and lips
and all around the stench
of half-digested fish
breathes over me.

JUST GUESSING . . .

The silkworm has eleven brains. It lives only on mulberry leaves, sheds its skin four times, and spins up to 300 yards of silk in a single cocoon. The moth lives for only two or three days and never flies – whatever its dreams!

The first tempts her
from black pre-birth night
at the heart of her egg.

The second makes her
a searcher of mulberry leaves,
drawn by green light.

With the third she learns to gnaw,
weaving between newly-shredded twigs;
in and out, out and in.

The fourth, fifth, sixth and seventh
nudge her into moults,
each one shed with an old skin.

Now she is well-fed,
but routine can drag
and memory wear thin.
The eighth and ninth
keep food in mind.

With the tenth
she learns to spin.
Untold yards of wedding silk
ceremoniously veil her head
until she sleeps,
returned once more
into a silken night.

And all this time
the last one dreams of light.
And in her dreams
she raises wings from darkness to the sun;
she raises wings at last
in grateful, glorious flight.

KANGAROO HAIKU

Out of the forest,
on to the dry plain you spring,
light with grassy dreams.

LATE

You're late, said miss.
The bell has gone,
dinner numbers done
and work begun.

What have you got to say for yourself?

Well, it's like this, miss.
Me mum was sick,
me dad fell down the stairs,
the wheel fell off me bike
and then we lost our Billy's snake
behind the kitchen chairs. Earache
struck down me grampy, me gran
took quite a funny turn.
Then on the way I met this man
whose dog attacked me shin –
look, miss, you can see the blood,
it doesn't look too good,
does it?

Yes, yes, sit down –
and next time say you're sorry
for disturbing all the class.
Now get on with your story,
fast!

Please miss, I've got nothing to write about.

LEARNING TO SWIM

Today I am
dolphin-over-the-waves,
roach and stickleback,
silver mermaid,
turning tide,
ribbon-weed
or sprat.

Water drifts through my mind;
I twist, I glide,
leave fear behind in sand,
wander a land
of turtle, minnow, seal
where whale is king.

Today – I swim!

LINES

I must never daydream in schooltime.
I just love a daydream in Mayshine.
I must ever greydream in timeschool.
Why must others paydream in schoolway?
Just over highschool dismay lay.
Thrust over skydreams in cryschool.
Cry dust over drydreams in screamtime.
Dreamschool thirst first in dismayday.
Why lie for greyday in crimedream?
My time for dreamday is soontime.
In soontime must I daydream ever.
Never must I say dream in strifetime.
Cry dust over daydreams of lifetimes.
I must never daydream in schooltime.
In time I must daydream never.

LORD NEPTUNE

Build me a castle,
the young boy cried,
as he tapped his father's knee.
But make it tall
and make it wide,
with a king's throne just for me.

An echo drifted on the wind,
sang deep and wild and free:
Oh you can be king of the castle,
but I am lord of the sea.

Give me your spade,
the father cried;
let's see what we can do!
We'll make it wide
so it holds the tide,
with a fine throne just for you.

He dug deep down
In the firm damp sand,
for the tide was falling fast.
The moat was deep,
the ramparts high,
and the turrets tall and vast.

Now I am king,
the young boy cried,
and this is my golden throne!
I rule the sands,
I rule the seas;
I'm lord of all lands, alone!

The sand-king ruled
from his golden court
and it seemed the wind had died;
but at dusk his throne
sank gently down
in Neptune's rolling tide.

And an echo rose upon the wind,
sang deep and wild and free:
Oh you may be king of the castle,
but I am lord of the sea.

MAGIC MIRROR

Step before the magic mirror,
tell me what you see.

Could it be
    me, stretched tall,
    unfolded, gaudy blanket,
    giant transfer
    ironed to the wall,
    a sprawl of paint
    splashed in a dull hall
    by a lonely stair?

Could it be
    some painted circus-clown
    blown from a nearby town,
    oil, marbled in a puddle,
    fuddled stained-glass window,
    Joseph's coloured coat,
    or splintered light
    from Noah's rainbow,
    low in a torn grey sky,
    after the storm?

Could it be
    Christmas crackers
    in wrappers tinselled
    and bright as a glass bauble,
    a summer garden
    dancing through rainy glass,
    waving flags, each one
    flown for a fair princess,
    or trembling wings
    of dragonflies,
    caught in August sun?

You look in the magic mirror,
tell me what you see;
is that really only – me?

MAKE YOUR OWN MONSTER: A DIY GUIDE

How do you make a monster?

Not with the glare of a torch-eye
slicing into the dark;
not with a gash of yellow paint
or the swing of a bat-wing cloak.
Nor with the roar of a dinosaur
or a sudden ruler-crack,
nor with egg-boxes, staples, glue . . .

This is what you do . . .

You lie awake after twilight
under a starless sky;
you leave your window just ajar
and feel the night creep by.
When the window squeaks
you start to sweat,
you remember the wind is still
and yet . . .
A creak in the hall
crawls on to the stair
and you know that somehow
something is there . . .

Your mouth is dry
and the hairs on your back
stand to attention,
stopped in their track.
And a shadow crouches
by the door . . .
gathers breath
then slowly creeps

across the floor

TOWARDS YOU!

Then, you can be sure
you've made your monster!

LONDON Z TO A

Zealous young xylophonists wait vacantly
under thundery skies,
rarely quiet,
playing on,
nightly.

Melodies lurk knowingly,
jingle, invade hearts,
glide from each deep corner,
begging answers.

MARIAGE À LA MODE

She made a good wife, my Aunt Sylvie.
With her curing hams and butter churn,
clocks glass-domed against a century's turn,
the waft of cooling milk or rising bread . . .
tight-lipped Victoria herself could earn
no better praise for thrift
or life well-led.

How would she see me now, piercing
with laser eye and sharper tongue
the wasted peelings, scribbled
'Try the freezer dear, must go!' . . .
fast-forward entrances and partings,
whilst the weeds and ironing grow?

Lean, tight-bunned
with coil of grey which never fell
(was she once a girl, Aunt Sylvie?)
even at rest she firmly rocked
behind pursed lip and needle-click,
knitting thick socks with love
and pleasure – of a kind.

How would she see
the ready beans, pale chickens
plastic-clad and featherless;
tin-opener, out-of-season lettuces
and packets of square fish?

Tempus fugit
glints her grey-faced clock.
Unseen, she fills the gloom
and watches, silenced
by the Hogarth prints.

MARY CELESTE

Only the wind sings
in the riggings,
the hull creaks a lullaby;
a sail lifts gently
like a message
pinned to a vacant sky.
The wheel turns
over bare decks,
shirts flap on a line;
only the song of the lapping waves
beats steady time . . .

First mate,
off-duty from
the long dawn watch, begins
a letter to his wife, daydreams
of home.

The Captain's wife is late;
the child did not sleep
and breakfast has passed . . .
She, too, is missing home;
sits down at last to eat,
but can't quite force
the porridge down.
She swallows hard,
slices the top from her egg.

The second mate
is happy.
A four-hour sleep,
full stomach
and a quiet sea
are all he craves.
He has all three.

Shirts washed and hung, beds
made below, decks done, the boy
stitches a torn sail.

The Captain
has a good ear for a tune;
played his child to sleep
on the ship's organ.
Now, music left,
he checks his compass,
lightly tips the wheel,
hopes for a westerly.
Clear sky, a friendly sea,
fair winds for Italy.

The child now sleeps, at last,
head firmly pressed into her pillow
in a deep sea-dream.

Then why are the gulls wheeling
like vultures in the sky?
Why was the child snatched
from her sleep? What drew
the Captain's cry?

Only the wind replies
in the rigging,
and the hull creaks and sighs;
a sail spells out its message
over silent skies.
The wheel still turns
over bare decks,
shirts blow on the line;
the siren-song of lapping waves
still echoes over time.

MIDAS

'The touch of gold!'
King Midas boldly craved.
Eyes glittered as he ran
from Bacchus' mountain cave
to find a golden land
where purple grape and twig of oak,
sleek lizard, stone and waving corn
like golden apples of the sun
all gilded to his stroke.

'A golden future!'
Midas cried
upon his golden throne.
And scarlet rose with olive branch,
plump aubergine and fragrant grass
passed through his grasping Judas kiss
to dazzle in the sun.

'Bring on the feast!'
King Midas laughed,
reached out for wine and bread;
raised his glass to take a sip
but when the red wine touched his lip
King Midas understood.

Oh gold was my corn and green my vine
and red was my wine of old;
never again shall I pine for wealth
or crave a richer world.

Lord Bacchus took pity, freed the king
from the gift he had longed to hold;
yet Autumn comes still with its Midas touch,
turns all to dying gold.

MIDNIGHT FOREST

Who wanders wild
in moon and puffball light
where night sleeps black
and spiders creep?
What is that sound
that stills the air?
Whose is the breath
that rustles oak and fir?
Beware,
the tree-gods stir.

MONKEY

I am
swing-on-a-tail,
up with the sun,
fast as white lightning
slits skies at noon.
Now under palms,
now over fern;
dawn-creeper, branch-leaper,
dive, twist and turn.
Face-in-the-forest,
chasing the moon;
tree-lover, sky-brother,
dew-dancing one.

MOSQUITO

I am
go-as-you-please,
easy houseguest;
I ask no fuss.
My one request,
a little space
to spread my wing.
No lace-edged tablecloth
or grand settee,
no silver dish
or cutlery . . .
Just you
and me.

I am
a simple pet.
I need no lead,
no need for kennel, collar,
cage or vet.
My gentle buzz
is far more sweet
than wasp's or bee's.
I'd never tease or groan,
or eat you out of house and home . . .
A little bite
is quite enough.

So why,
please tell me why
        . . . ?

MOTH

Fly-by-night,
moon-brusher,
searcher of light;
flibbertigibbet,
translunar kite.
Now a leaf,
now a message,
silent in flight:
wisp of torn paper
that drifts out of sight,
then lifts in the wind
and is lost
to the night.

MR. ALLPORT'S JACKET

*(For the poets of ALL ages at Parsons Down Junior
School, Thatcham!)*

We all dressed up
for the poetry night:
poet in her velvet best,
pupils starched in Persil white;
mums in skirts and polished boots,
teachers all inspection-smart;
governors in smooth grey suits,
head, as always, just the part.

Smiles slid round the darkened hall:
each poet dazzled, head to feet
as they slowly rose and gave their all ...
But *no-one* could compete

with Mr. Allport's jacket!

Where DID you get it, sir?
What did MRS. Allport think?
Did you think you'd grow to fit it?
If you wash it it MIGHT shrink!

Its very .. . UNUSUAL, sir . . .
did you get it in the sale?
*Did you see the colour in **DAY**-light?*
Was it REALLY on the rail?

Mr. Allport gave a mysterious smile,
as proud as a two-tailed bear.
I'M a poet too, he said.
But all we could do was stare . . .

at Mr. Allport's jacket!

MUM'S INFALLIBLE METHOD FOR SOLVING ARGUMENTS ABOUT WHO GETS THE BIGGEST SLICE OF CREAM CAKE

I'll make sure
no-one loses;
you cut,
she chooses!

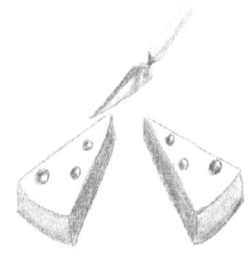

MUSIC LESSON

I know this piece.
I've played it every night,
struggled, contorted hands,
until I barely knew
fingers from thumbs,
black notes from white.

I know this piece.
It may sound trite
but I'd worked hard
and learnt it through.
I knew the score.
I played it well last night.

I know this piece,
yet when we reach the day . . .
dismay. I cannot play.
I blush and mutter,
fingers stutter over notes,
the music flies away.

I knew this piece –
but that was yesterday.

NEW BEGINNINGS

You're starting school! my mother said.
You'll read and write and sew . . .
But I can read at home, I cried.

Big girls all go!

You'll love the boys and girls, she said,
and all those games they play . . .
But I could stay and play at home!

Big girls don't stay!

I stood and stared through wooden gates,
and watched her wave good-bye,
till sudden mist hid her from view . . .

Big girls don't cry!

NIGHT

There's a dark, dark wood
inside my head
where the night owl cries;
where clambering roots
catch at my feet
where fox and bat
and badger meet
and night has eyes.

There's a dark, dark wood
inside my head
of oak and ash and pine;
where the clammy grasp
of a beaded web
can raise the hairs
on a wanderer's head
as he stares alone
from his mossy bed
and feels
the chill of his spine.

There's a dark, dark wood
inside my head
where the spider weaves;
where the rook rests
and the pale owl nests,
where moonlit bracken
spikes the air
and the moss is covered,
layer upon layer,
by a thousand fallen leaves.

ONCE . . .

Long moons ago
in a silver dawn
around the time
when the stars were born
a beautiful horse
with a twisted horn
as smooth as silk
but sharp as a thorn
danced out of the mist
towards the sun . . .

and the dew-bright horse
with the twisted horn
that first danced then
when the stars were born
danced in the name of
u n i c o r n,
long moons ago
in that new-world dawn.

ORANG-UTAN

Watch me,
touch me,
catch-me-if-you-can!
I am
soundless,
swung-from-your-sight,
gone with the wind,
shiver of air,
trick-of-the-light.

Watch me,
touch me,
catch-me-if-you-dare!
I hide, I glide,
I stride through air,
shatter the day-star dappled light
over forest floor.
The world's in my grasp!
I am windsong,
sky-flier,
man-of-the-woods,
the arm of the law.

PARTNERS

Find a partner,
says sir, and sit
with him or her.
A whisper here,
a shuffle there,
a rush of feet.
One pair,
another pair,
till twenty-four
sit safely on the floor
and all are gone
but one
who stands,
like stone,
and waits;
tall,
still,

. . . alone.

PERSEPHONE

Lay down your poppies
    red with sun,
    beneath the judas-tree;
    beware the black-horsed lord of night,
    Persephone.

Bury your violets
    with the shades,
    drink deep the black, black sea;
    ferry your corn to Dis's cave,
    Persephone.

Fasten your veil with
    lilies pale,
    dull nightshade dim your eyes;
    under sad lilac make your grave,
    till winter dies.

PETER'S TALE

Life was not easy.
On some days fish
leapt in profusion to our nets,
sun-silvered in the early light;
at other times storm-winds
riled angry waves to battle
and we longed for land,
or nets were hauled in almost empty
to the waiting shore.
It was not always easy
but familiar, known, secure.

That morning, as we cast our nets,
there was no force,
no need to follow;
yet we followed,
without question, sure.

It was not
just the steady gaze
through sun-deep eyes
reflecting rising hills and sea;
not just the voice
that filled the waiting air
with calm and certainty;
nor just the stance,
the look that spoke of otherworlds
beyond the shores of Galilee
and yet . . .

We followed,
drawn invisibly,
forever changed;
both prisoner
yet free.

PICNIC

George, lend a hand
and spread that cloth.
the sand is everywhere!
Just look at that,
you'd never think
it took hours to prepare!

WAKE UP, GRAMP!
Your food's all out,
get it while you can!
Have a lemonade before
it warms up in the sun.

What is it, Mum?

There's . . .

ham with sand,
and spam with sand,
there's chicken paste
and lamb with sand;
oranges, bananas,
lemonade or tea;
bread with sand
all spread with sand –
at least the sand comes free!
We've crisps with sand
and cake with sand –
it's grand with lunch or tea –
crunch it up,
enjoy it, love,
at least we're by the sea!

POLAR CUB

This way, that way?
Step out,
little five-toe flat-foot,
squint-eye,
cave-dazed,
into the sun!

Eyes left,
ears right,
nose to the wind!

The coast is clear!
Run, roll, lollop;
winter's done!
Enjoy the pause;
make your mark
on this blank page –
the world is yours!

POMPEII
24th August, A.D. 79

The giants are sleeping now
under a hot land
where the grey snow
has yet to fall
and cover all
with its dying dew.

The city is silent now
under a haze of blue
till the pedlar's cart
on the stone-clad street
calls the early few
for pot or shoe
and the slave from sleep.

The hillside is sunwashed now
where the lush vine
and the olives line
the summer slopes
of the giants' home
in an August dream
that has almost gone.

The gods are sleeping now
unaware
by the temple walls
and market stalls
of the city square . . .

And an ashen cloud
shrouds the breathless crowd
as the grey snow falls.

PUFFING BILLY

Puffing Billy, built in 1813, is probably the world's oldest locomotive. It is on permanent exhibition at the London Science Museum.

Sometime-dinosaur,
rattling hulk of bones
that lumbered once
through English green,
spelt death to ancient ways
in smoke-black breath.

Now anchored
on a one-way track to nowhere,
Penny Black of steam;
collected, shown
for all to gawp and say:
He had his day,
those early engine-makers
knew their stuff.

Now silenced, still,
his last breath gone:
Tyrannosaurus Bill
run out of puff.

RAP-A-BYE BABY

Ali love to tap-dance when dem drums all beat,
An' when dat rhythm start you never catch those feet
'cos he's a tipper-tapping, snipper-snapping dancing
     man
an' he can dance de world away like no other dancer
    can.

Ali love to tap-dance when dem trumpets blow,
An' when dat rhythm start you have to watch him go
'cos he's a tipper-tapping, snipper-snapping
flipper-flopping, slipper-slopping dancing man
an' he can dance de world away like no other dancer
    can.

Ali love to tap-dance when dem clarinets play,
An' when dat rhythm start you know him miles away
'cos he's a tipper-tapping, snipper-snapping,
flipper-flopping, slipper-slopping,
clapper-clipping, bipper-bopping dancing man
an' he can dance de world away like no other dancer
    can.

He can dance de world away like no other dancer can;
he can dance de world away although he only in his pram!

REJECTION

The travellers, weary now in every pore
with eyes downcast beneath the darkening sky
still wait in silent hope outside the door.

The inn is full; they've seen it all before.
We've no room here! and then a brusque *Goodbye!*
to travellers weary now in every pore.

In disbelief, too tired to implore,
they try to turn away but wonder why
they wait in silent hope outside the door.

Rejection is not easy to endure;
where *can* you go when there's no place to lie
for travellers weary now in every pore?

The landlord hesitates, becomes unsure,
now sensing a despair he can't pass by;
they wait in silent hope outside the door.

The stable? Could he offer only straw
with lowing cattle for a lullaby?
The travellers, weary now in every pore,
wait still in silent hope beside the door.

RHINOCEROS

There is no rush.
I have slept away
centuries of midday sun,
brushed folded skin
through canes and banyan,
hoof-toed through still grass
with eyes half-closed
to the healing mud
of ancient swamps.
Centuries are mapped on my forehead;
I am not of this time.
My horn beckons . . .

ROOM AT THE INN

Draughty, husband, that stable.
She looked . . . warm, though.
Almost at home.
And you know, husband, I swear
it's not one mite as dark in there
as you'd have thought.
And that child - so still, so quiet.
Perhaps they'll need more straw?
It won't get any warmer, early hours.
Maybe we should bring them in?
Husband, you're not listening!

There is our bed . . .
but then with breakfast early
and so many travellers . . .
Well, *they* won't go tomorrow, surely?
Husband, did you see . . . ?
Husband!
Oh well, old man, dream on!
Some day we've had,
and then those two arriving,
with every nook and cranny gone!

Funny how those moths
circled the old lantern,
husband. Almost like . . .
almost as if those three . . .
but no, it couldn't be!
And the light,
you should have seen the light!
Oh, it flickered, but
so bright, so bright,
and night so still.
Draughty it is, that stable,
husband.

SATURDAY NIGHT BLUES

What could be worse
than an empty purse?

SCIENCE, 1953

It was called Domestic Science then.
Formica no more heard of than moon travel,
Beatles, tights or Home Econ.,
each wooden table must be scrubbed
(scrubbed hard and long)
after each shapeless pasty,
limp cucumber sandwich,
had earned its sad D+
from school, and later home.
To me they tasted fine.

Miss explained that only *tops*
of frying pans required a shine,
as blackened bottoms drew more heat.
Highly scientific, so we thought,
but not my mother.
Slapdash and dirty, she's a fool,
my mother muttered, crossly
brandishing wire wool.

She was not noted for her scientific flair;
I less still for my domestic skill.
Yet three domesticated decades on
I live with blackened proof
that science won.

SEA DREAM

I wander the deep-sea forests
where the snake-fish slither;
where the dark dunes drift
like rolling mist
and the white whales murmur.

I wake to coral blossom
and sleep in a star-clad cave;
my bed is a glade
of ribboned jade,
my sky a wave.

I dance by the spiny urchin
and ride the giant clam;
I feel as I sail
the dolphin's tail
the sad whale song.

SEALSONG

Around me, seas
stretch endlessly;
above me, sky.
A space to breathe,
a place to swim;
to pace the days
by moon or sun.
A place that time
had kept from man;

no place to die.

SEA SONG

Come sail the whispering seas, my love,
Come drift on the tides with me;
For I still long for the wild waves' song
And the silver fish of the sea.

Oh I'd sail the sighing seas, my love,
Where the wild weeds gently glide;
But I'm afraid of the forest shade
Where the silent fishes hide.

Don't fear the sauntering seas, my love,
As they dance beneath the breeze;
In the moonlit foam we'll make our home
Like the silver fish of the seas.

Oh I'll sail the rolling seas, my love,
And sigh for the cry of the wind;
But what if I weep on the ocean deep
To tread a greener land?

Oh you'll love the roaring seas, my love!
Come ride the swell with me,
Where the breaking sky is drawn to die
With the silver fish of the sea.

If I ride the raging seas, my love,
Then will you follow me?
Or will you stay till your dying day
With the silver fish of the sea?

Oh I must ride the wild, wild seas
And you must let me be;
Till my dying day I'll roam the spray
With the silver fish of the sea.

SEASON SONG

Spring stirs slowly, shuffles, hops;
Summer dances close behind.
Autumn is a jostling crowd
but Winter creeps into your mind.

SEARCHER

Princess, what are you dreaming,
down among the moist rushes?

Soft pleated linen, beaded bracelets,
purple grapes, and Pharaoh's finest wines
await you at the palace –

yet you follow a wavering baby's cry.

SEVENTEEN THINGS TO DO WITH A BABY
For Paul

Watch
his eyes
watch your eyes,
search out his mother's face,
follow other faces;
wonder who he'll recognise.

Feel
his fingers
monkey-grip your finger,
feet frog-kick against your hand;
wonder when he'll stand.

Talk to him!
Chatter, recite, hum!
Watch his tongue curl,
lips part and close;
he knows already
how to listen.
Whistle, whisper, say anything;
sing him a nursery-rhyme
and wonder when, one day,
he'll start to sing.

Listen!
He sucks like any Hoover,
noisy as a new-born calf
or toddler with his first straw,
unwilling to stop;
wonder when he'll drain *his* cup
greedily, to the final, noisy drop.

Wonder.

SLICK MONSTER

Velvet black wave
gently laps the shore;
small white seagull
flies no more.

Shiny black monster
slowly creeps to land;
small pink crab
buried in the sand.

SNOW DREAMS

Snow slides over hill and forest,
ices rooftops,
muffles the land.

Behind the white-cloaked fir,
remembering his childhood,
an old man hides
in silence,
snowball in hand.

SOMETHING TO DO IN A TRAFFIC JAM

Dream of
a world where
bat and tiger wander free
and turtles set their courses by
the stars.

SONG OF THE FROG PRINCE

It's the royal bed I miss.
Oh, I can do without
the state occasions,
the bowing and the handshakes,
the gold crown, weighting my head.
All those unwanted presents
to be grateful for,
and far too many strawberries,
out-of-season.
But the royal bed . . .
pillows, soft with silk,
deep, feathered mattresses
with satin sheets,
quilts billowing with eider.

A kiss, dear lady, please.
Just one small kiss.

SOUNDS OF SILENCE?
(A riddle)

My words fill your head
like a chattering tongue,
though I'm mute as a marble,
silent as stone.

I cheer you or sadden,
puzzle or preach;
entertain you, persuade you,
amuse you or teach.

Paperweight, motionless,
soundless as bone . . .
yet though speechless,
not spineless: I carry
a weight of my own.

Choose me now, use me,
then set me down:
never fear, I'll be there

when you are long gone!

(A book!)

SOUTH WITH SCOTT

Here white is not absolute.
Beyond the groaning of the sledge
it rises through eerie silences
in countless characters,
a trickster with his myriad disguises
haunting each man's journey, day and night. . .

The spectral white of ice through fog
ghosts its way, unreal, towards invisible horizons
where a southern ocean must meet land
and land meet cloud;
the loud blaze of white
that fiercely scoops up light from snow,
hurls it blindingly at stinging eyeballs.
Ahead, rock-white fringes the next glacier,
a great glittering river of blue-white
caught briefly in December sun.
Frozen breath cobwebs our beards
in near-translucent white,
bridal-veiled eyes peer
for blue-black chasms
lurking underfoot.

White unfolds around us to infinity,
a pale blank page:
sometimes folded, crumpled,
sometimes notepad-smooth,
attendant always on
the printing of our tale.

In this white wilderness
there is no place to hide;
wind snatches breath,
claws into cheeks,

prises eyelids wide.
Even in fitful sleep
a wraith-like white drifts,
then lies, persistently,
behind closed eyes.

No more than restless shadows
on the endless white
we flounder,
marking time,
awaiting only now
the closing of this Polar night.

SPACESHIP EARTH

I am . . .

space-dancer,
drawn to the light like a moth;

an ancient coin
spun through night air;

silver penny,
lost in a deep pocket;

small change,
cast on a dark cloth –
a wager on life . . .

Spend me
if you dare!

SPIDER'S SONG

See, I have stitched the ivy
with beaded threads of light,
a rich embroidery, newly hung.
Step on my tightrope,
lie with me;
let me fold you tenderly
in my pearled hammock,
lull you to silken sleep,
sweet dreamer,
under the dying sun.

S.S. TITANIC
15th April, 1912

First was the silence. Not below,
where silver forks and laughter
chink in each saloon;
where layered decks of dance and song
echo through perfumed corridors,
all set to last till dawn.
Nor several tiers down
in simpler quarters.
There, for the first time ocean-borne,
emigrants still chatter,
more subdued in tone;
entrust to some far-off new world
their dreams
and all they own.

But high above the deck
is peace.
The wind is slight,
though air has chilled surprisingly:
little swell,
no waves to speak of,
movement smooth, unhampered.
The theatre set.
Viewed from the gods her course is clear,
pulled, as if by chains, on steady track
towards her destination.
Behind, the wake spreads endlessly,
stretches wide then slowly fades
into the night.

Only a faint jarring interrupts
that almost total silence of the sea,
barely noticed by the revellers.

There is no panic.
A brief encounter with an icy shelf
means nothing to a ship that is
unsinkable . . .

Later, she begins to list;
the rest is known.
Emigrants from flooded cabins
claw through dark companionways,
held back to save the rich;
lifeboats lowered quarter-full;
the shameless fights for precedence.

And for the rest,
gathering in disbelief on darkened decks,
the wait.
One weeps,
one lights a cigarette,
one goes below, changes to evening dress
to meet his fate.
On sloping decks the band play on –
Hold me up in high waters
their almost final line.

At last, she rises almost vertical –
a lifelong memory
for those who lived to tell the tale –
then slides, nose-first
towards her brave new world
encompassed only by
the lasting silence of the sea,
the silence of the sky.

STABLE SONG

She lies, a stillness in the crumpled straw
Whilst he looks softly on the child, unsure,
And shadows waver by the stable door.

The oxen stir; a moth drifts through the bare
Outbuilding, silken Gabriel-winged, to where
She lies, a stillness in the crumpled straw.

A carpenter, his wife, both unaware
That kings and shepherds seek them from afar
And shadows waver by the stable door.

The child sleeps on. A drowse of asses snore;
He murmurs gently, raises eyes to her
Who lies, a stillness in the crumpled straw.

A cockerel crows, disturbed by sudden fear
As shepherds, dark upon the hill, appear
And shadows waver by the stable door.

The hush of birth is in the midnight air
And new life hides the distant smell of myrrh;
She lies, a stillness in the crumpled straw,
And shadows waver by the stable door.

STIRRING TIMES

Families weren't small.
Isabella Beeton
could rustle up a meal
just starting with

the head of a hog,
a pint of cream,
two dozen eggs . . .

and still know
that nothing would be left
uneaten.

STORYTIME

Once upon a time, children,
there lived a fearsome dragon . . .

Please, miss,
Jamie's made a dragon.
Out in the sandpit.

Lovely, Andrew.
Now this dragon
had enormous red eyes
and a swirling, whirling tail . . .

Jamie's dragon's got
yellow eyes, miss.

Lovely, Andrew.
Now this dragon was
as wide as a horse
as green as the grass
as tall as a house . . .

Jamie's dragon would JUST fit
in our classroom, miss!

But he was a very friendly dragon . . .

Jamie's dragon ISN'T, miss.
He eats people, miss.
Especially TEACHERS,
Jamie said.

Very nice, Andrew!
Now one day, children,
this enormous dragon

rolled his red eye,
whirled his swirly green tail
and set off to find . . .

His dinner, miss!
Because he was hungry, miss!

Thank you, Andrew.
He rolled his red eye,
whirled his green tail,
and opened his wide, wide mouth
until

Please, miss,
I did try to tell you, miss!

SUNFLOWER

Guards my south wall,
a private sun.
Floodlights the whole garden,
warms tardy flowerbeds into life
in leafy July.

She turns to face the sun – we're told;
I know it's wrong.
Really the sun chases my Inca goddess,
jealous of rival gold.

THE COMING OF THE WELL

Our fields have gone,
the days burn on;
Cry for the sigh of the rains!

The days burn on;
beneath that sun
Long for the lash of rain!

Beneath the sun
with swollen tongue
Beg for the roar of the rain!

With swollen tongue,
though no words come
Pray for the whisper of rains!

Though no words come
and days burn on,
beneath our land,
still crazed by sun,

Hear the song of the rains!

*Though no rains come
and days burn on,
beneath our land
we hear that song;*

*Hear the song of the rains.
Dance to the song of the rains!*

THE DARE

Go on, I dare you,
Come on down!

Was it *me* they called?
Pretend you haven't heard,
a voice commanded in my mind.
Walk past, walk fast
and don't look down,
don't look behind.

Come on, it's easy!

The banks were steep,
the water low
and flanked with oozing brown.
Easy? Walk fast
but don't look down.
Walk straight, walk on,
even risk their jeers
and run . . .

Never go near those dykes,
my mother said.
No need to tell me.
I'd seen stones sucked in
and covered without trace,
gulls slide to bobbing safety,
grasses drown as water rose.
No need to tell me
to avoid the place.

She ca-a-a-n't, she ca-a-a-n't!
Cowardy, cowardy custard!

There's no such word as 'can't',
my father said.
I slowed my pace.
The voices stopped,
waited as I wavered, grasping breath.
My mother's wrath? My father's scorn?
A watery death?

I hesitated then turned back,
forced myself to see the mud below.
After all, it was a dare . . .
There was no choice;
I had to go.

THEN

They never expected it of my grandmother,
all this choice.
Stolid, vocationally-trained
with neat samplers and clear instructions on
pastry-making and how to preserve the strawberries,
for forty years she happily baked my grandfather
rabbit pie, brawn, haslet;
collected fresh farm milk,
still-twitching pullets
and their warm muck-splattered eggs,
manure for the rhubarb, and mushrooms
dawn-gathered in chill Lincolnshire fields.

THE OVER-REACHER

You can do anything, my father said;
A challenge to my childish pride, no threat.
His words will blindly dog me till I'm dead.

For forty years enmeshed within my head
I carried this and cast out far my net.
You can do anything, my father said.

Searching, unsatisfied by daily bread
I sweated on, unwilling to forget;
His words will blindly dog me till I'm dead.

My body gave a caveat: just tread
With caution, you can't walk on water yet.
You can do anything, my father said.

Becalmed in doldrum age, no longer fed
With pestering pride he rests; for me the debt.
His words will blindly dog me till I'm dead.

How many years I wished those words unsaid;
Too late to change, may flesh still live to fret.
You can do anything, my father said;
His words will blindly dog me till I'm dead.

THE ROMANS IN BRITAIN
(A history in 40 words)

The Romans gave us aqueducts,
fine buildings and straight roads,
where all those Roman legionaries
marched with heavy loads.

They gave us central heating,
good laws, a peaceful home . . .
then after just four centuries
they shuffled back to Rome.

THE SNOWMAN'S PRAYER

May cool breezes blow
on my snow-dancing face;
may rain stay away
and leave me in place.

May my body shine brightly
whilst winter is here;
may I dance in the sun then
and melt without fear.

SONG-THRUSH

Slug-slayer, snail-snatcher,
soprano turned percussionist,
mad drummer of the rock;
now executioner,
still centre-stage,
beats out her dizzy solo
on execution block.

THE PURPOSE OF KEEPING A TORTOISE

A tortoise
is not a pet I long to keep.
In Summer?
All he does is eat and crawl.
In Winter?
Hide and sleep!

THE WORM'S TALE

'*Women from St Teresa's Cheshire Home near Penzance,*
Cornwall, beat 34 other teams in the 10th annual worm
charming championships yesterday at Blackawton, South
Devon. Three of the night staff managed to lure 72 worms
from their 12 ft. square plot in the 15 minutes allowed.
"The secret of our success was the worm song we sang
constantly and the cold tea we poured on the ground," said
Ms Allan, team captain . . .'

The Guardian , May 1993.

Dew sinks through the darkness,
dissolves like snow
into this private land of night.

I am no stranger to the gloom.
Here below
my pace is measured:
a gracious minuet
danced between roots of bindweed.
Here I could weave for ever
the dark fabric of my life;
here I could stay.

I have felt before
earth shake as thunder rolls,
the steady fall of rain on stone.
I have no fear.

And yet, today
I am aware of something
more insistent than a storm,
more haunting than a shower;
a watery almost-spell,
calling . . .

I turn,
lifted by music;
drawn, like Lazarus,
from the night.
Slowly I twist and rise
towards the day;
slowly I spiral out of darkness
into light.

TIGER

Tiger, eyes dark with
half-remembered forest night,
stalks an empty cage.

TIMELESS

There is no clock in the forest,
but a dandelion to blow,
an owl that hunts
when the light has gone,
a mouse that sleeps
till night has come,
lost in the moss below.

There is no clock in the forest,
only the cuckoo's song
and the thin white
of the early dawn,
the pale damp-bright
of a waking June,
the bluebell-light
of a day half-born
when the stars have gone.

There is no clock in the forest.

TONGUE IN CHEEK

My heart's in my mouth,
my brain has been washed –
my tongue's in my cheek.

I've a chip on my shoulder,
I've brought up a child –
I'm feeling quite weak.

I've paid through the nose,
made a pig of myself –
you should take a peek.

I'm pulling a face,
here's a piece of my mind –
I really can't speak.

My eyes are the size
of three stomachs or more –
my tongue's in my cheek.

TWO-WEEK HOLIDAY DIARY OF MAN OF FEW WORDS

13th August	England.
14th August	Rain again.
15th August	Plane.
16th August	Spain.
17th August	Sun.
18th August	Fun.
19th August	Sea.
20th August	Sand.
21st August	Sea.
22nd August	Fun.
23rd August	Sun.
24th August	Spain.
25th August	Plane again.
26th August	Rain.
27th August	England.

UFO DIY

Umbrella Fights Officer?
Unapproachable Fish Offside?
Uncanny Frog Objects?

Unfold Furled Omelette?
Unattached Fabulous Oarsman?
Underpants Fumigate Oldham?

Try your own DIY UFO Poem!

upside down, unlikely
united, uncle, uncanny
uncertain, ultimate,
unbolt, underpants,
unbeaten, unbutton
unaware, unassuming
unapproachable, unable
umbrella, under, ugly
unattached, ultimate
unwind, unscramble
unmentionable, uncork
unconscious, unlikely
underground, unique
undeveloped, unfold,
understand,
underground
unfreeze, unbeaten
unzip, uproarious
upgrade, unskilled
underwater, undress
underarm, umpire
ukelele, ulcers
unicycle, unmask, use
usher, utensil, unload
upset, U-turn
ungovernable

fade, fish,
fashionable, fabric
fabulous, face, facts
fiddle, fail, fair, fare
fat, fall, false, fame
feel, faint, ferocious
fit, fill, film, fine,
find, fix, first,
fighting, free, fritter,
frog, fry
fuse, funnel, fuzzy
futuristic, fun, flood,
flatten, fly, fume,
follow, foggy, front
frequently, frizzle
flibberty-gibbet
first, formidable
forlorn, foreign
French, foolish
foreboding, force
forget, forge, forfeit
fraudulent
film, Filofax
flummoxed fumigate,
form, foul
frolic, friendly,

obligation, oak,
oath, oarsman
oar, oatmeal
obedient, obelisk
obesity, oboe
observation, oil
obnoxious, ode
obscure, okapi
observant, ocean
obsession, offer
obsolete, obstacle
obstinacy, office
obvious, occasion
occupation, other
occupant, October
octuplets, oddball
odd, offence
official, offside
offshore, offspring
okay, Oldham
Olympic,
omelette
one-stop, ozone
ooze, opposite
onomatopoeia
outrageous

UNIDENTIFIED   FLYING   OBJECT

UNCLE WILLIAM

I stayed with you once
in your tiny church-lane cottage
with the outside pump, the velvet cloth
and sing-songs cramped around the piano.

With black-fringed stumps of fingers,
braces, ample paunch,
you could have been
miner, dustman, sweep –
but no; village blacksmith
fitted best that village scene.

I remember strong green soap,
tin bowls of icy water for the morning wash;
my aunt's night-calling for the cat
across still hedgerows and the cobbled lane,
a shared bed with spoiling cousins,
Billy Bunter by oil lamp at forbidden hours
and orange moths against the darkened pane.

Uncle William. Dead now;
the blacksmith and the cottage gone.
No cobbled lane but just a road now,
a road my aunt must tread alone.

VILLAGE SCHOOL

A stile, a field,
some dozen cows
and then the church.
A muddy dyke,
some silver roach
and just below the bridge
a sharp-toothed pike
which lurks alone
for small unwary stragglers,
whispering doom.

The school, one room.
Beneath high-windowed stone
fixed smiling in her chair
the kindly Mrs. Mullins,
large in blue and black
with neatly-curlered hair.
From nine to twelve
and later on till three
she calls our fate
and welcomes all
on ample knee.
A scratch of slate,
a shuffle here or there,
a child in late;
chalk-dusted autumn
clouds the air.

At last a break. Wait
unwillingly for bottled milk,
cool in its rattling crate,
then under teacher's watchful eye
lace-up for play.
Scarves, coats and hopscotch

when the weather's dry
and crying at the gate for home
under a grey Lincolnshire sky.

VOICES IN MY HEAD

I daren't!

You can do it.

I can't!

You can do it.

What if . . . ?

You can do it.

Perhaps . . .

You can do it.

DARE I do it?

You can do it.

Well, MAYBE I should . . .

You can do it.

I DID IT!

I said you could do it.

I knew I would!

WHALESONG

I am
ocean-voyager,
sky-leaper,
maker of waves;
I harm no man.

I know
only the slow tune
of turning tide,
the heave and sigh
of full seas meeting land
at dusk and dawn,
the sad whale song.
I harm no man.

WHAT IS ONE?

One is the sun,
a rhino's horn;
a drop of dew,
a lizard's tongue.

One is the world,
a lonely whale;
an elephant's trunk,
a monkey's tail.

One is an acorn,
one is a moon;
one is a forest,
felled too soon.

WHAT ON EARTH?

What on earth are we doing?
Once wood-pigeons flew,
and young badgers tunnelled
where oak and ash grew . . .

Now the forest's a runway,
and all that flies through
is a whining grey plane
where the pigeons once flew.

Where on earth are we going?
At the end of the lane
once blackberries hung
in soft autumn rain . . .

Now the lane is a car park,
and never again
will fruit fill our baskets
down in the lane.

Why on earth are we crying?
Once morning dew shone
on hawthorn and primrose,
caught in the sun . . .

Now the forest is carpeted
only with stone.
No primrose, no hawthorn;
the forest has gone.

WHEN *I* WAS A GIRL . . .

There was no supermarket.
Milk was carried in a can,
from Uncle George's farm;
mushrooms were gathered from fields,
butter churned in Aunt Sylvie's scullery.

There was no television.
All the family sang around the piano;
children sat on any willing knee
for nursery rhymes and tales
'til dusk darkened the small parlour.

Water bubbled on the open fire,
children and adults bathed in front of it.
And then, as silence wrapped the village,
oil lamps led the way to bed
through eerie shadows . . .

So my Granny said.

WINTER

Winter crept
through the whispering wood,
hushing fir and oak;
crushed each leaf and froze each web –
but never a word he spoke.

Winter prowled
by the shivering sea,
lifting sand and stone;
nipped each limpet silently –
and then moved on.

Winter raced
down the frozen stream,
catching at his breath;
on his lips were icicles,
at his back was death.

WOLF

Still on his lone rock,
stares at the uncaged stars and
cries into the night.

WOODLOUSE

Armoured dinosaur,
blundering through jungle grass by
dandelion-light.

Knight's headpiece, steel-hinged,
orange-segment, ball-bearing,
armadillo-drop.

Pale peppercorn, pearled
eyeball; sentence without end,
my rolling full-stop.

ACKNOWLEDGEMENTS

With many thanks to –

John Foster, who first took some of my early poems for some of his excellent anthologies.

Brian Moses, who kindly prodded me to gather a new collection after I'd reached a rather large birthday!

Loren Ryland-Epton and John Chandler for their generous time and effort in unravelling a rather unruly manuscript!

Some of these poems first appeared in *Magic Mirror, Midnight Forest, and Dragonsfire* by JN (all published by Faber & Faber); *Wish You Were Here?* and *Storm's Eye* by JN (Oxford University Press), and in numerous anthologies over many years. The copyright for all individual poems is mine.

Judith Nicholls
3 May 2022

ABOUT THE AUTHOR

Brought up in her grandmother's Lincolnshire cottage during World War Two, **Judith Nicholls** has lived in Wiltshire since 1970. Her first collection of poems, *Magic Mirror*, was published by Faber in 1985, and she has written or compiled more than forty poetry collections for children; her poems have also appeared in hundreds of anthologies. Judith sees poetry as pattern, understanding, exploration, exhortation and explanation. Her interest has always remained in crafting words, in finding echoes in the poems. In many hundreds of visits to schools, she would always unfold the sequence of the drafts that usually preceded the smallest poem.

Although her poems are still to be found in many anthologies, Judith's books are now largely out of print, so it has been lovely, she says, to have been able to make a selection from them for Hobnob Press.

Hobnob Press has a growing list of titles by West Country poets.
For details explore our website, www.hobnobpress.co.uk, from which you may order copies of these and other Hobnob Press publications.

Lightning Source UK Ltd.
Milton Keynes UK
UKHW020823300922
409689UK00009B/489